# The Classic Tradition
# of Haiku

## AN ANTHOLOGY

DOVER · THRIFT · EDITIONS

# The Classic Tradition of Haiku

## AN ANTHOLOGY

EDITED BY
**FAUBION BOWERS**

**DOVER PUBLICATIONS, INC.**
Mineola, New York

## DOVER THRIFT EDITIONS

GENERAL EDITOR: STANLEY APPELBAUM
EDITOR OF THIS VOLUME: STEVEN PALMÉ

*Copyright*

Copyright © 1996 by Faubion Bowers.
All rights reserved.

*Bibliographical Note*

*The Classic Tradition of Haiku: An Anthology* is a new work, first published by Dover Publications, Inc., in 1996.

*Library of Congress Cataloging-in-Publication Data*

The Classic tradition of haiku : an anthology / edited by Faubion Bowers.
    p.     cm. — (Dover thrift editions)
  ISBN-13: 978-0-486-29274-8
  ISBN-10: 0-486-29274-6
  1. Haiku — Translations into English.    I. Bowers, Faubion, 1917–    II. Series.
PL782.E3C53    1,96
895.6'1008 — dc20                                                        96-13877
                                                                            CIP

Manufactured in the United States by Courier Corporation
29274609
www.doverpublications.com

# Contents

# Foreword

The question, "What are haiku?" is more often asked than answered. Westerners have described haiku (pronounced evenly *hi-koo*) as epigrams, snapshots or telegrams. Sir George Sansom (1883–1965) defined them as "little drops of poetic essence." Harold Henderson (1889–1974), who made haiku a part of our own literature, dubbed them "meditations . . . starting points for trains of thought." R. H. Blyth (1898–1964), who published six volumes of haiku translations, made the extravagant claim that "Japanese literature stands or falls by haiku."

Historically, haiku stem from twelfth-century *renga* (literally "linked songs" or "linked verses" — the word for poem and song in Japanese is the same), an elegant literary pastime in which poets, singly or in groups, improvised connecting stanzas to create long poems of up to 10,000 verses. *Renga* were interlocking chains of 17 syllables (5-7-5), preceded or followed by 14 syllables (7-7), with each tercet and couplet producing a poem in itself.

In the sixteenth century, the traditional arts truly rose in popularity among the common people. Along with Kabuki theater and *ukiyo-e* (woodblock prints), *haikai-no-renga* raged as a national fad. *Haikai*, from two words meaning "sportive" and "pleasantry," meant unusual or offbeat and is translated (somewhat deceptively) as "comic linked verse." It was a reaction to the formality of the "language of the gods" used in the *waka* / *tanka* of Court poesy, written by rarified *mikados* and later, as power shifted from the nobles to the military, by exalted shoguns and ruling warriors. *Haikai* spoke in everyday language and sometimes, in its exuberance, became little more than a display of wit and scatology.

By the second half of the seventeenth century, the genius-poet Bashō and his followers elevated *haikai* to a level of great sensitivity and dignity, although the underlying humor and surprise often remained present. During this period, the opening 5-7-5 stanza of *renga*, called *hokku* or "starting verse," became independent, what William J. Higginson calls "stand-alone verse." By poetic fiat, the *hokku* had to contain a seasonal word (*kigo*) and be an entity complete unto itself. Bashō himself never heard the word *haiku*; it has only come into vogue in the twentieth century. *Hai* in *haikai* means "unusual" and *ku* denotes strophe, lines, stanza or verse. Recently, *hokku* and *haiku* have become interchangeable.

The Haiku Society of America, founded in 1968, spent two years and used some 200,000 words in letter exchanges among authorities before reaching a dictionary definition for haiku. They are the world's shortest poems, consisting of 17 syllables arranged in a sequence of 5-7-5. An example, written in English by the poet James Kirkup, demonstrates the 5-7-5 syllabic pattern:

> Haiku should be just
> small stones dropping down a well
> with a small splash

In Japanese, haiku comprise as few as three or, at most, ten words, but translation into English often requires many more.

The Japanese language has 50 sounds: 5 short and long vowels (long vowels count as two syllables in haiku) that can combine with 14 consonants. By contrast, English has 20 consonants that combine with 6 vowels. All Japanese words end in a vowel, except for a few ending in a slightly nasal "n" (counted as one independent syllable).

Rhythmically, Japanese falls into measures of five and seven syllables. These single word- or phrase-lengths flow as naturally as iambs or trochees do in our more strongly accented English. Novels, Kabuki dramas and thousand-stanza poems have been written in the alternating 5-7 (or 7-5) syllabic system.

There is much discussion but little agreement among scholars as to whether haiku should be transcribed in one, two or three lines. In Japan haiku are usually printed in one vertical column but, when handwritten on poem cards, they often appear in three columns, making visible the 5-7-5 syllabic impulse.

Arthur Waley (1865–1966), an early translator of Japanese literature, wrote, "It is not possible that the rest of the world will ever realize the importance of Japanese poetry, because of all poetries it is the most completely untranslatable." To our way of thinking, Japanese poetry lacks sentence structure. It is imprecise in articles, particles, plurals and gender, and uses neither capital letters nor punctuation. Rhyme is easy and monotonous and, therefore, something to be avoided. Japanese, even with its limited number of basic sounds does, however, lend itself to an abundance of wordplays — double entendre, puns, assonances, alliterations, frontal rhymes and onomatopoeia.

In all their brevity, haiku do tell a story and paint a vivid picture, leaving it up to the reader or listener to draw the meanings out and complete them in the mind's eye. Many poets embellished their writing with shorthand, brush-stroke drawings. Each haiku also contains a hidden dualism: the near and the far, foreground and background, then and now, past and present, high and low, sound and silence, and temporality and eternity.

Haiku lovers look for specific words and images to help reveal the deeper layers of meaning that expand the scope of each poem. These fall into three general categories: What, Where and When.

The "what" is the poet's reaction to something affecting one or more of the senses: sight (swirling petals or falling leaves); hearing (the sound of a waterfall or the tumble of a scarecrow after the harvest); scent (the faint aroma of plum blossoms or of a wilted chrysanthemum); and even taste (the tang of a persimmon or the delicate freshness of the season's first eggplant).

The "where" can be a particular place redolent with connotations and associations such as the ancient capital of Nara, Mt. Fuji or the exile island of Sado. "Where" can also be as vague as an unnamed pond, a road or an inn.

The most evocative part of haiku is "when." Many haiku presuppose a time of year, month or day. The place in time of the poem is often conveyed by references to occurrences in nature or to specific flora and fauna. Haze connotes spring; clouds, summer; mist or fog, autumn. A frog denotes late spring; plum is the first flower of the New Year; wisteria blooms in late spring and morning glories in summer.

Whether or not one knows the language, haiku cannot be truly appreciated without some attention to the original sounds. It is useful to note the *kireji* (cutting word), meaningless syllables such as *ya, kana, zo, yo,* or *keri*. Although haiku are "songs" to be uttered in one breath, the cutting word introduces a minute caesura or thought-pause for emphasis. In Japanese it occurs often on the fifth or twelfth syllable, and breaks the tiny poem asymmetrically. In English, translators convey the idea by punctuation marks (!, —, . . . , and :) or by expressions such as "Ah," "Lo" or "Behold."

There are an estimated one million haiku writers in Japan today. Most newspapers run haiku sections to which subscribers submit poems for comment. Scholars deliver hour-long lectures on the meanings of just one of these 17-syllable poems. Stones with haiku carved in them dot the cities and countryside and commemorate places where laureates, past and present, have paused during long journeys seeking poetic inspiration from the landscape. In no other country is poetry more deeply respected, or so pleasantly ubiquitous.

# Acknowledgments to Translators

Each translation in this anthology is followed by the initials of the translator. The following list, arranged in alphabetical order by initials, identifies each translator and, when applicable, the work from which his translations were taken.

**AG**   Allen Ginsberg. *Collected Poems 1947–1980*. New York: Harper-Collins, 1984.

**AK**   Alex Kerr. *Lost Japan*. Melbourne, Australia: Lonely Planet Publishers, 1996.

**AM**   Asatarō Miyamori (1869–1952). *One Thousand Haiku: Ancient and Modern*. Tokyo: Dōbunsha, 1930.

**BHC**   Basil Hall Chamberlain (1850–1935). "Bashō and the Japanese Poetical Epigram." *Asiatic Society of Japan*, vol. 2, no. 30 (1902).

**BLE**   Bernard Lionel Einbond, Professor of English Literature at Lehman College, City University of New York.

**BW**   Burton Watson, former Professor of Japanese and Chinese at Columbia University. *From the Country of Eight Islands*, by Hiroaki Sato and Burton Watson. New York: Doubleday, 1981.

**CAC**   Cheryl A. Crowley, Professor of Japanese at Columbia University. "Putting *Makoto* into Practice: Onitsura's *Hitorigoto*." *Monumenta Nipponica*, vol. 50, no. 1 (1995).

**CHP**   Curtis Hidden Page (1870–1946). *Japanese Poetry*. Boston: Houghton Mifflin, 1923.

**CMW**   Clara M. Walsh. *Master Singers of Japan*. London: John Murray, 1910.

**DF**   Dallas Finn. *Meiji Revisited: The Sites of Victorian Japan*. Trumbull, CT and New York: Weatherhill, 1995.

**DK**   Donald Keene, Professor Emeritus of Japanese at Columbia University. *Landscapes and Portraits*. Tokyo: Kodansha, 1971. / *World within Walls*. New York: Holt, Rinehart and Winston, 1976.

**EGS**   Edward G. Seidensticker, Professor Emeritus of Japanese at Columbia University. "When Mugwort Last in the Dooryard Bloomed." *Japan Quarterly*, Jan.–Mar. (1962). / *Very Few People Come This Way*. Brighton, England: In Print, Ltd., 1995.

**EK**   Eleanor Kerkham, Associate Professor of Japanese at the University of Maryland.

**EM**   Earl Miner, Professor of Japanese at Princeton University. *Japanese Linked Poetry*. Princeton, NJ: Princeton University Press, 1979.

**FB**   Faubion Bowers.

**GWB**  Glen William Baxter, former Professor of East Asian Studies at Harvard University.

**HGH**  Harold Gould Henderson (1889–1974). *An Introduction to Haiku*. New York: Doubleday, 1958.

**HS**  Hiroaki Sato, president of the Haiku Society of America (1979–1981). *One Hundred Frogs*. New York and Tokyo: Weatherhill, 1983. / *From the Country of Eight Islands*, by Hiroaki Sato and Burton Watson. New York: Doubleday, 1981. / *Bashō's Narrow Road*. Berkeley: Stone Bridge Press, 1996.

**IMo**  Ivan Morris (1925–1976), trans. *The Life of an Amorous Woman*, by Saikaku. Norfolk, CT and New York: New Directions, 1963.

**IMu**  Ian Mutsu, president of the International Motion Picture Co., Tokyo.

**IN**  Inazō Nitobé (1862–1902), former Professor at Tokyo Imperial University, 1893.

**JB**  Janice Brown, Professor of Japanese at the University of Alberta.

**JBe**  Janine Beichman, Professor of Japanese Literature, Daitō Bunka University, trans. *A Poet's Anthology*, by Ooka Makito. Santa Fe: Katydid Books, 1994. / [Author] *Masaoka Shiki*. Tokyo: Kodansha, 1982.

**KY**  Kenneth Yasuda. *The Japanese Haiku*. Boston and Tokyo: Tuttle, 1957.

**LH**  Lafcadio Hearn (1850–1904). *Japanese Lyrics*. Boston: Little and Brown, 1900.

**LK**  Laurence Kominz, Professor of Japanese at Portland State University. "Danjūrō V and Kabuki's Golden Age," [Booklet]. Portland Art Museum, October, 1993. / *Three Pioneer Kabuki Actors and Their Legacy Today*. Tokyo: Kodansha, 1996.

**LM**  Lewis Mackenzie, trans. *The Autumn Wind*. Tokyo: Kodansha, 1930.

**MB**  Max Bickerton. "Issa's Life and Poetry." *Asiatic Society of Japan*, Second Series, vol. IX, Dec. (1932).

**MM**  Mark Morris, Professor of Japanese at Trinity College, Cambridge. "Buson and Shiki." *Harvard Journal of Asiatic Studies*, vol. 44, no. 2 (1984) and vol. 45, no. 1 (1985).

**MU**  Makoto Ueda, Professor of Japanese at Stanford University. *Matsuo Bashō*. Tokyo: Kodansha, 1970. *Bashō and His Interpreters: Selected Hokku with Commentary*. Stanford: Stanford University Press, 1992. (Reprinted with the permission of the publishers, Stanford University Press. © 1992 by the Board of Trustees of the Leland Stanford Junior University.)

**NGS**  Nippon Gakujutsu Shinkōkai (Japan Society for the Promotion of Science). *Haikai and Haiku*. Tokyo: Nippon Gakujutsu Shinkōkai, 1958.

**PD & YI**  Patricia Donegan, Fulbright Senior Research Scholar, and Yoshie Ishibashi, translator and researcher for the Museum of Haiku Literature, eds. and trans. *Chiyo-ni: Woman Haiku Master*. Boston and Tokyo: Tuttle, 1996.

**RBF**  Richard B. Finn, former U. S. State Department Officer.

**RHB**  Reginald Horace Blyth (1898–1969). *Haiku*. 4 vols. Tokyo: Hokuseidō Press, 1949–52.

**SDC**  Steven D. Carter, Professor of Japanese at the University of California at Irvine. *Traditional Japanese Poetry: An Anthology*. Stanford: Stanford

University Press, 1991. (Reprinted with the permission of the publishers, Stanford University Press. © 1991 by the Board of Trustees of the Leland Stanford Junior University.)

**SF**   Soichi Furuta. "Haiku: An Art for All Seasons." *Japan: An Illustrated Encyclopedia*. Vol. 1. Tokyo: Kodansha, 1993.

**SG &**   Sanford Goldstein, former Professor of American Literature at Keiwa
**SS**   College, Shibata, Japan, and Seishi Shinoda, Professor Emeritus at Niigata University, Niigata, Japan. *Songs from a Bamboo Village*, by Sanford Goldstein and Seishi Shinoda. Boston and Tokyo: Tuttle, 1996.

**SHJ**   Stanleigh H. Jones, Jr., Professor of Japanese at Pomona College, Claremont, CA.

**SN**   Shigeru Nishimura (1828–1933), former Tutor at Gakushuin University, Tokyo, 1879.

**TGT**   Toshio G. Tsukahira, former U.S. Foreign Service Officer.

**TR**   Thomas Rimer, Professor of Japanese at the University of Pittsburgh. Introduction to *From the Country of Eight Islands*, by Hiroaki Sato and Burton Watson. New York: Doubleday, 1981.

**WGA**   William George Aston (1841–1911). *A History of Japanese Literature*. New York: D. Appleton, 1899.

**WJH**   William J. Higginson. *The Haiku Seasons*. Tokyo: Kodansha, 1996. / *The Haiku Handbook: How to Write, Share, and Teach Haiku*, by William J. Higginson with Penny Harter. New York: McGraw-Hill, 1985, and Tokyo: Kodansha, 1989. (The translations appearing are by William J. Higginson. Copyright © 1985 by William J. Higginson. Reprinted by permission of the translator.)

# Iio Sōgi (1421–1502)[1]

*yuki nagara / yamamoto kasumu / yūbe kana*[2]

Snow yet remaining
The mountain slopes are misty—
An evening in spring

DK

Despite some snow
the base of hills spreads with haze
the twilight scene

EM

*morokoshi mo / ame shita to ya / tsurakaran*[3]

Does not China also
lie beneath this selfsame sky
bound in misery

EM

---

[1] Paragon of *renga* (linked verse) masters. Sōgi was of humble origins, so much so he kept his birthplace secret. However, as a great poet, he moved in the highest circles. The Kamakura Shogun appointed him Administrator of the Bureau of Renga Contests in Kyoto, a poet's highest official honor.

[2] Perhaps the most famous *hokku* in *renga* literature, written in 1488 when Sōgi was 67. It alludes to a poem written two-and-a-half centuries earlier by Emperor Go-Toba, a patron divinity of poets, and opens the *renga* sequence, "A Hundred Stanzas by Three Poets at Minase." Go-Toba once had a palace at Minase, not far from the capital of Kyoto.

[3] These linking verses of 5-7-5 and 7-7 are excerpted from Sōgi's *renga* "A Hundred Stanzas by Sōgi Alone," written in 1499 at age 79. Sōgi called this solo *renga* "a record of my world and lifetime." A curiously autobiographical masterpiece, it expresses despair at the helplessness of the Emperor in the face of fierce civil wars then raging.

1

### *sumeba nodokeki / hi no moto mo nashi*[1]

yet even in the sun's own land
anyone who lives will suffer
EM

### *yama kawa mo / kimi ni yoru yo o / itsuka min*

shall we ever see
the time your reign brings lasting peace
to all hills and streams
EM

### *ayafuki kuni ya / tami mo kurushiki*

and will the land not fall in ruin
with its commoners in distress
EM

### *iyashiki mo / mi o osamuru wa / aritsubeshi*[2]

Among the lowborn too
must be some who spend their time
in tranquillity.
SDC

---

[1] The word for Japan, being to the east of China, is written in two ideograms meaning "origin" and "sun," hence the well-worn cliche "Land of the Rising Sun."
[2] Sōgi refers to his own low social status, as well as to his search for inner peace through self-discipline. This is the penultimate stanza of "Three Poets at Minase."

However low one may be
it is in holding oneself in sway
that is imperative

EM

*yo ni furu mo / sara ni shigure no / yadori kana*[1]

passing through the world
indeed this is just
a shelter from the shower

WJH

*mono goto ni / oi wa kokoro no / ato mo nashi*

everything that was
has vanished from my aged heart
leaving not a trace

EM

---

[1] Poets traveled in search of inspiration, enduring hardships and dangers. In the early winter drizzle (*shigure*), shelter for himself and his poems was urgent. *See* Buson, p. 55.

## Sōchō    (1448–1532)[1]

### Sōgi: *nao nani nare ya / hito no koishiki*

### Sōchō: *kimi o okite / akazu mo tareo / omou ran*[2]

What could be the cause of it —
that I should feel such love again?
            While I still have you,
            why think of anyone else?
            Why this discontent?

                    SDC

•–•

For what reason can it be
that you should seem so dear
            apart from you
            who else appeals forever
            and holds my love

                    EM

## Yamazaki Sōkan    (1464–1552)[3]

### *koe nakaba / sagi koso yuki no / hitotsurane*[4]

If only noiseless they would go,
The herons flying by
Were but a line of snow
Across the sky

                    CHP

[1] "Three Poets at Minase" was composed by Sōgi and two of his disciples: Sōchō, a blacksmith's son, and Shōhaku, a nobleman and son of a Minister of State. The entire work was written in six hours, with each poet inventing a stanza every three minutes.

[2] At certain junctures in *renga*, love or yearnings (*omoi*) had to be touched on before moving to other pre-designated topics of poetic converse. The master Sōgi here poses a riddle: Why do I love when already I love? Sōchō caps his master's verse cleverly by referring to the enigma of infidelity. Sōchō became a priest at 17 but, despite a vow of celibacy, formed various liaisons with women who bore him children.

[3] Page to an Ashikaga Shogun and an important founder and anthologizer of *haikai no renga*.

[4] Generally considered to be Sōkan's masterpiece. *Sagi* is a white heron or egret.

### *tsuki ni e o / sashitaraba yoki / uchiwa kana*[1]

O Moon! — if we
Should put a handle to you,
What a fan you'd be!

HGH

### *te o tsuite / uta mōshiaguru / kawazu kana*[2]

hands to the floor
offering up a song
the frog . . .

WJH

O thou obsequious frog,
With hands spread on the ground,
And croaking flatteries of such solemn sound.

CHP

### *waga oya no / shinuru toki ni mo / he o kokite*[3]

Even at the time
When my father lay dying
I still kept farting.

DK

---

[1] *Uchiwa* is a flat, round fan as opposed to *ogi* or *sensu*, the folding fan, which a Japanese court lady invented in the 12th century.

[2] Sōkan half-mocks samurais' prostrations before their masters.

[3] This famous stanza was written in answer to the 7-7 "challenge" or "riddle": Bitter it was / but also funny (*niganigashiku / okashikari keri*). Sōkan's solution was criticized, not for being "below the neck," as Bashō would later define scatology, but for violating the Confucian ethic of filial piety, or respect for one's parents.

# Arakida Moritake    (1472–1549)[1]

*rakka eda ni / kaeru to mireba / kochō kana*

A fallen blossom
  returning to the bough, I thought —
But no, a butterfly.
   SDC

*aoyagi no / mayu kaku kishi no / hitai kana*[2]

  Green willows
Paint eyebrows on the face
  of the cliff
   CAC

*asagao ni / kyō wa miyuran / waga yo kana*[3]

My span of years
Today appears
  A morning-glory's hour.
   CHP

---

[1] Chief priest at Ise Shrine (Shintō) who also popularized *haikai no renga* in his later years.
[2] Refers to the custom for women to shave their eyebrows and paint in arched ones.
[3] Written on his deathbed at age 75. It was also his birthday.

# Matsunaga Teitoku (1571–1653)[1]

*mina hito no / hirune no tane ya / natsu no tsuki*[2]

> For all alike
> the cause of noontime napping
> is the summer moon
>
> EM

*setsugekka / ichido ni miyuru / utsugi kana*[3]

> It lets one see
> Snow, moon, and blossoms — all at once.
> oh, *utsugi!*
>
> HGH

*kesa taruru / tsurara ya yodare no / ushi no toshi*[4]

> This morning, how
> Icicles drip! — Slobbering
> Year of the Cow!
>
> HGH

---

[1] Teitoku's poetry, now neglected, made *haikai* a part of the legitimate poetic canon.

[2] Another version of this poem says *aki no tsuki* (autumn moon). The idea is that the full moon is so beautiful that people of refinement stay up all night staring at it and composing poems. The next day, they sleep.

[3] Japanese fancy trinities of favorite things — snow, moon and flowers, for one. Here, in May moonlight, the tiny white flowers of the shrub *utsugi* (*Deutzia scabra*) gleam like snow.

[4] A New Year's Day verse ushering in the Year of the Cow. Bashō disparaged Teitoku and called his poetry "slobber." He objected to his facility and the analogy of dripping icicles to a ruminant's slaver.

# Matsue Shigeyori [Ishū]    (1596–1670)[1]

### *yaa shibaraku / hana ni taishite / kane tsuku koto*[2]

Hey there, wait a moment,
Before you strike the temple bell
At the cherry blossoms.

DK

# Yasuhara Teishitsu    (1609–1673)[3]

### *kore wa kore wa / to bakari hana no / yoshino yama*[4]

Uttering only
"Oh! Oh! Oh!" I roam over
Yoshino hill ablow.

IN

•-•-

Look at that! and that!
Is all I can say of the blossoms
At Yoshino Mountain.

DK

[1] Disciple of Teitoku and first teacher of Onitsura. *See* Onitsura, p. 37.

[2] In Japan, the lifespan of a cherry flower is only three days and the poet fears the bell's reverberation will cause the petals to fall sooner than they should.

[3] One of Teitoku's "Five Stars" or disciples. Teishitsu destroyed all but three of his 3,000 *haikai* poems, leaving us with less than 30 of his words.

[4] Bashō called this "the finest *hokku* ever written." Mt. Yoshino, a large hill in Southern Japan, has four groves of 100,000 white mountain cherry trees. For three days in early April the hill billows with intense whiteness. Note the irregular six-syllable first line.

# Nishiyama Sōin   (1605–1682)

### ikani ikani / hana mo koyoi no / tsuki ichirin

No, no, not even the cherry blooms,
can equal the moon of tonight.

AM

### sake hitotsu / nodo tōru ma ni / tsuki idete[1]

While a shot of saké passes the throat, the moon appears

HS

### hototogisu / ikani kijin mo / tashika ni kike[2]

'Tis the cuckoo —
Listen well!
How much soever gods ye be!

WGA

---

[1] Rice wine (*saké*) invariably accompanied festivities. *Tsuki idete* can also be interpreted as a pun for an erection.

[2] *Hototogisu*, translated as cuckoo, wood thrush and sometimes even nightingale, is virtually synonymous with haiku. It is a black-breasted bird speckled with white dots, has green legs and its open mouth is a bright blood red. It lays eggs in the nest of the nightingale (*uguisu*). It winters in South Asia, migrates to Japan in May and stays until autumn. It sings day or night, particularly in bright moonlight, even when flying. The song is a strong but mournful cry — *coo-coo-coo*, uttered twice. It is said to die after singing 8,008 times. *Hototogisu* is also known as the "bird of time," "messenger of death" and "bird of disappointed love," and flies back and forth from this world to the next.

*yo no naka ya / chōchō tomo are / kaku mo are*[1]

Life
Is like a butterfly
Whatever it is.

AK

## Ihara Saikaku    (1642–1693)[2]

*kokoro koko ni / naki ka nakanu ka / hototogisu*[3]

Is my mind elsewhere
Or has it simply not sung?
Hototogisu

DK

*tai wa hana / wa minu sato mo ari / kyō no tsuki*[4]

Villages may lack
Sea bream or flowers
but they all have tonight's moon.

AK

---

[1] This refers to Chuang Tsu (Zhuangzi; 369–289 B.C.), the eccentric Chinese Taoist scholar, who dreamed he was a butterfly. When he awoke he wondered if he was a butterfly dreaming he was a man.

[2] Became Sōin's pupil at age 14. Saikaku was an exemplar of erotic writing and a pioneer of popular fiction and detective stories in Japan. A *haikai* master, legend has it he once composed 23,500 verses in 24 hours.

[3] Saikaku's earliest known stanza. It refers to the Confucian axiom "If one's mind is elsewhere, one will look but not see, listen but not hear," as well as to the rarity of the *hototogisu*. Note the "k" sounds in Japanese. The haiku imitates the bird's call. *See* note 2, p. 9.

[4] *Tai*, sea bream or red snapper, is a large, succulent fish, an expensive delicacy for gourmets and a good-luck symbol.

*Yoshiwara de / budō shōri o / ezaru koto*[1]

In the Yoshiwara
The way of the warrior
Cannot conquer

IMo

*ukiyo no tsuki / misugoshini keri / sue ninen*[2]

I have gazed at it now
For two years too long—
The Moon of the Floating World.

IMo

I had two last years
of extra gazing at
The moon of the Floating World.

AK

## Yamaguchi Sodō   (1642–1716)

*me ni wa aoba / yama hototogisu / hatsugatsuo*[3]

A view of greenery,
a wild cuckoo,
the first bonito

EGS

---

[1] In the "Nightless City" or pleasure district of Edo (Tokyo), commoners such as Saikaku and samurai were equals in buying or vying for the favors of women.

[2] Saikaku's last poem, written at age 52. At that time life expectancy was 50 years for a man, so Saikaku had an extra two years in his world of ephemeral pleasures.

[3] One of the most famous of all haiku. Unusually, it includes three "seasonal words" (*kigo*). It tells of the trio of splendid summer enjoyments for eye, ear and tongue. Bonito or skipjack is a small, greatly relished tuna, especially when it first comes into season.

*yado no haru / nani mo naki koso / nani mo are*[1]

In my hut this spring,
There is nothing—
There is everything!

RHB

*ume no kaze / haikai koko ni / sakan nari*[2]

A plum scented wind
In the land of haikai
Blows triumphant.

DK

## Ichikawa Danjūrō I    (1660–1704)

*shigamitsuku / satogo ya toko no / kirigirisu*[3]

Is it a foster child clinging to me?
The cricket in my bedding.

LK

[1] A celebration of poverty; the joy of spring unencumbered by possessions (other than those of barest necessity).

[2] Written during a poetry session with his friend Bashō. Bashō's 7-7 answering link was:

> *kochitozure mo / kono toki no naru*
> Even for the likes of us
> This is the spring of the age.    DK

The two men express their joy at the popularity of *haikai* poetry writing.

[3] The great Kabuki actor was alone, performing in Kyoto. He was accustomed to his three children crawling in under his *futon* (quilts), but he had sent them back to Edo with his pregnant wife. Now, in his loneliness, he imagines himself a wet nurse to a cricket, an autumn insect of sadness.

# Kitamura Kigin    (1623–1705)

*natsuyase to / kotaete ato wa / namida kana*[1]

"Oh my thinness is caused by summer heat,"
I answered, and burst into tears.

AM

**••••**

"Summer thinness dear,"
I replied to him, and then
could not check a tear.

KY

# Hōjō Dansui    (1662–1711)

*miyuki ni mo / amigasa nuganu / kagashi kana*[2]

The scarecrow does not uncover
Even to His Imperial Majesty.

AM

# Matsuo Bashō    (1644–1694)[3]

*bashō uete / mazu nikumu ogi no / futaba kana*[4]

Having planted a plantain, at once I hate two stalks of reed

HS

---

[1] Titled "Secret [or Hidden] Love." Kigin, an important literary figure, taught Bashō.

[2] "Uncover" means to remove one's hat in the presence of a superior.

[3] Bashō is the most significant writer in haiku history. He was designated a god in the Shintō pantheon in 1793.

[4] In 1681, a pupil gave him a banana or plantain plant (*bashō*), while the poet was living in a simple house. The rare plant thrived and became "king of the garden," quickly reaching the height of the roof. During the course of his life, Bashō used some 15 pen names. By age 38, in 1682, he was so fond of the banana tree he began using the signature "Bashō." He likened himself to the plant: it had neither use nor beauty; in temperate Japan its fruit was inedible; in wind or rain, the broad leaves shredded like "phoenix tails;" the trunk, too soft for lumber, resembled "dragon scales." *Ogi* is a weed-like reed so rank it chokes neighboring growths. Bashō, noted for his gentleness, rarely expressed dislike for any part of nature.

I plant a banana tree
But first see only two stalks
Of dreaded weeds.

AK

by my new banana plant
the first sign of something I loathe —
a miscanthus bud

MU

*kareeda ni / karasu no tomari keri / aki no kure*[1]

On dead branches crows remain perched at autumn's end

HS

on a barren branch
a raven has perched —
autumn dusk

WJH

On a leafless bough
A crow is sitting: — autumn,
Darkening now —

HGH

[1] Bashō's first masterpiece (1681) and probably the Japanese poem most influential on the English language. It inspired Imagism, notably Ezra Pound's renowned 1914 poem, "In a Station of the Metro" and, in 1917, Wallace Stevens' masterly "13 Ways of Looking at a Blackbird," a series of haiku derivations in English. *Karasu* is an ominous bird, different from a crow, raven, rook or blackbird, as it is variously translated. Bashō drew three pictures to accompany this *hokku*. One shows seven "crows" on a branch while 20 others are wheeling in the sky. Two later paintings depict a single bird resting on a lifeless tree limb, and one shows a lively bird aflutter.

*furuike ya / kawazu tobikomu / mizu no oto*[1]

Old Pond — frogs jumped in — sound of water

LH

•-•-

A lonely pond in age-old stillness sleeps . . .
   Apart, unstirred by sound or motion . . . till
Suddenly into it a lithe frog leaps.

CHP

•-•-

The quiet pond
      A frog leaps in,
            The sound of water

EGS

•-•-

old pond . . .
a frog leaps in
water's sound

WJH

•-•-

Th'old pond — a frog jumps in. Kerplunk!

AG

•-•-

frog pond : . .
a leaf falls in
without a sound

BLE[2]

[1] Bashō's most quoted *hokku*, considered the apogee for manifesting "eternity in tranquility." Zen adepts take it to be symbolic of "instant wisdom" (*satori*). The last two lines were composed first, in 1682. Kikaku, the disciple, suggested the first line should read *yamabuki*, since these mid-spring wild yellow roses were then blooming near the fishpond outside Bashō's hut, and in classical poetry "frog" and "*yamabuki*" were a designated combination. See note 2, p. 16.

[2] In 1987, Japan Air Lines sponsored a Haiku in English contest. Poet Bernard Lionel Einbond won the Grand Prize over 40,000 other American and Canadian entries with this original poem.

### *inazuma ni / satorenu hito no / tōtosa yo*[1]

A flash of lightning
but still benighted
Oh worthy man!

FB

### *horohoro to / yamabuki chiru ka / taki no oto*[2]

Do the yellow-rose petals
Tremble and fall
At the rapid's roar?

NGS

### *umi kurete / kamo no koe / honoka ni shiroshi*[3]

The waters fade
and the wild ducks' cries
are faintly white

JBe

---

[1] "Lightning" suggests the sudden enlightenment (*satori*) achieved by Zen masters. Here Bashō, in *haikai*'s perverse fashion, is happy *not* to gain transcendence from a flash in the sky.

[2] *Yamabuki*, one of haiku's most frequently mentioned flowers, is translated as "yellow rose," "globe flower" and "kerria rose." Literally, "mountain blossom," it is a shrub of the rose family with delicate, luminous yellow petals, like a buttercup's, that turn white before scattering. In haiku it is associated with water.

[3] Note the irregular 5-5-7 form. Bashō could have transposed the lines but chose not to.

*hiru neburu / aosagi no mi no / tōtosa yo*[1]

> sleeping at noon
> the body of the blue heron
> poised in nobility
> EM

*shizukasa ya / iwa ni shimiiru / semi no koe*[2]

How still it is!
Stinging into the stones,
The locusts' trill.
DK

Quietness: seeping into the rocks, the cicada's voice
HS

*yagate shinu / keshiki wa miezu / semi no koe*

Never an intimation in all those voices of *sémi* . . .
How quickly the hush will come . . . how speedily all must die.
LH

> It gives no sign
> that it knows its death is near
> the cicada's cry
> EM

---

[1] Earl Miner sees this verse as a symbol of enlightenment. The bird dreams of a higher reality and yet, when noon passes, it will be recalled to the temporal world.

[2] Some versions begin with the words "mountain temple," the place where Bashō wrote the poem. Another variant starts with "loneliness" instead of "quietness." Japan has 30 species of cicada, locust or cricket, some of which are greatly prized for their "song" or chirr. *Semi* sing in midsummer; crickets, in autumn.

*matsushima ya / ā matsushima ya / matsushima ya*[1]

Matsushima!
Ah, Matsushima.
Matsushima!

FB

*shimajima ya / chiji ni kudakete / natsu no umi*

Islands: shattered into thousands of pieces in the summer sea

HS

*ominaeshi / sono kuki nagara / hana nagara*[2]

The *ominaeshi*, ah!
The stems as they are,
The flowers as they are.

RHB

---

[1] Bashō once said, "When you face splendid scenery, you become too entranced to make a poem." His second attempt was more explicit. Matsushima (literally, "Pine Island[s]," near Sendai in the north, is the most famous of Japan's many scenic wonders. In an area 12 miles wide, some 800 large and small islands are densely forested with thousands of pine trees whose branches, blown by salty sea winds, are twisted into millions of different shapes. *See* Teishitsu's inarticulate response to Mt. Yoshino, p. 8. Sodō gave this *hokku* to Bashō when Bashō set out on his famous journey to the North:

*matsushima no / matsu kage ni futari / haru shinan*
In the pine shade of Matsushima, the two of us shall die in spring   HS

[2] Another example of Bashō's "speechlessness" at the "Ah-ness" of things. *Ominaeshi*, a five-syllable word like *hototogisu*, permeates haiku history. According to Hiroaki Sato, it is one of the "Seven Flowers (or grasses) of Autumn." It grows to a height of three or four feet and the flowers have a soft, dewy appearance. When it blooms, its grain-like yellow flowers resemble millet, goldenrod or tiny forsythia. The word is sometimes translated as "harlot flower," "lady lily," "maiden flower" or occasionally, since *omina* can mean "old woman," as "old woman's meal."

### *kumo oriori / hito ni yasumuru / tsukimi kana*

Clouds now and again
give a soul some respite from
moon-gazing — behold

BLE

clouds occasionally
make a fellow relax
moon-viewing

WJH

### *yoku mireba / nazuna hana saku / kakine kana*[1]

Looking closely
I find a shepherd's purse blooming
under the hedge.

SF

### *michinobe no / mukuge wa uma ni / kuware keri*[2]

The roadside thistle, eager
To see the travellers pass,
Was eaten by the passing ass!

CHP

---

[1] *Nazuna* is a weed of the mustard family with tiny, four-petaled white flowers. The poem exemplifies "paying attention to the inconspicuous."

[2] Considered to be one of Bashō's pastoral masterpieces. Some interpret it as a moral, like the proverb "the nail that sticks out gets hammered down." *Mukuge*, "rose of Sharon" or "mallow," is a species of hibiscus, a hedge that can grow ten feet in height. Its hollyhock-like white blossoms are called "flower-of-the-hour," because they open in morning light and close in shade. They bloom in late summer.

Mallow flowers
By the side of the road —
Devoured by my horse.

DK

*mezurashi ya / yama o ideha no / hatsunasubi*[1]

How rare, How lovely!
    emerging from sacred peaks
        young Ideha eggplant

EK

*araumi ya / sado ni yokotō / ama no gawa*[2]

A surging sea . . .
reaching over Sado Isle
the Galaxy

SF

the rough sea —
flowing toward Sado Isle
the River of Heaven

MU

[1] *Ideha* means "coming out" and is also the name of a religious training ground. A priest at the temple honored Bashō with a gift of the season's first eggplant, a delicacy.

[2] Written while visiting Japan's west coast, looking at the turbulent nighttime sea. Bashō follows the blurry arch of the Milky Way (*ama no kawa*) and imagines it leads to the distant penal island of exiles, Sado. This, one of Bashō's most powerful poems, places man within the universe's vastness and heartbreak, an example of infinity contained within haiku compression. Shiki, who often criticized Bashō as "overrated," considered this *hokku* to be "sublime."

*natsukusa ya / tsuwamonodomo ga / yume no ato*[1]

Summer grasses
where stalwart soldiers
once dreamed dreams
>                    MU

The summer grass!
'Tis all that's left
Of ancient warriors' dreams
>                    IN

Old battle-field, fresh with spring flowers again
>    All that is left of the dream
Of twice ten thousand warriors slain.
>                    CHP

*rakugaki ni / koishiki kimi ga / na mo arite*[2]

Among these graffiti is the name of someone I love
>                    HS

Among the graffiti
The name of
Beloved you.
>                    AK

---

[1] Harold Henderson called this "the most discussed haiku in the language." It was written at Takadachi Castle where Lord Yoshitsune fought valiantly but vainly against his jealous brother's army in the twelfth century. The battle site was overgrown with weeds. Bashō wept at the memory of vanquished Yoshitsune and the vainglory of past heroism. Donald Keene sees the genius of the poem in its astonishing pattern of ahs, oohs and ohs with only one e:

*a-u-u-a-a / u-a-o-o-o-o-a / u-e-o-a-o*

[2] Technically not a *hokku* since it lacks a seasonal word (*kigo*).

*kimi ya chō / ware ya sōshi no / yume gokoro*[1]

You are the butterfly,
And I the dreaming heart
   of Sōshi?

RHB

*shirageshi ni / hane mogu chō no / katami kana*[2]

For the white poppy
the butterfly breaks off its wing
as a keepsake

MU

*botan shibe / fukaku wakeizuru hachi no / nagori
   kana*[3]

How reluctantly the bee emerges from
The depths of pistils of a peony!

AM

---

[1] Sōshi is the Japanese pronunciation of Chuang Tsu (Zhuangzi). *See* Sōin, note 1, p. 10.

[2] Bashō sent this verse to his young pupil Tokoku, who was exiled by the Shogun for fraud, "selling empty rice," (taking money for goods he did not possess). This poem is startling for Bashō, who rarely expressed "passion." Scholars see it as homoerotic, particularly since Bashō once wrote: "There was a time I trod the path of love for young boys (*wakashū*)."

[3] This was sent to another pupil, Toyo. It contains the longest second line in Bashō's poetry with 11 instead of 7 syllables.

*tsuki sumu ya / kitsune kowagaru / chigo no tomo*[1]

The moon is clear—
I escort a lovely boy
frightened by a fox

MU

*kochira muke / ware mo sabishiki / aki no kure*[2]

Will you turn toward me?
I am lonely too,
this autumn evening

MU

*hamaguri no / futami ni wakare / yuku aki zo*[3]

A clam
        separates lid
                from flesh as autumn departs

HS

---

[1] Written at a *renga* party when the subject of love was proposed. The picture here is of the aged Bashō walking home a catamite who has been frightened by a fox. Superstition had it that foxes assume the form of beautiful women at night. *Chigo* (altar boy or acolyte) was slang for a homosexual.

[2] A Zen priest gave Bashō a self-portrait with his face averted from the viewer. Bashō jokes, by asking the subject to move.

[3] Hiroaki Sato calls this "the most *haikai* of all pieces in *Narrow Road to the Interior*." This is the final poem of the travelog. Bashō again touches on separation from friends.

*shiragiku no / me ni tatete miru / chiri mo nashi*

A white chrysanthemum
Hold it before your eyes
No dust.

AK

The white chrysanthemum
When lifted and looked at
Remains pure

RBF

*kono michi ya / yuku hito nashi ni / aki no kure*[1]

Along this way
No travellers.
Dusk in autumn.

AK

*tabi ni yande / yume wa kareno o / kakemeguru*[2]

Fallen sick on a trip
Dreams run wildly
Through my head.

DF

Ill on a journey
All about the dreary fields
Fly my broken dreams

EGS

---

[1] Ill and old, Bashō wonders if his disciples will continue his *haikai* tradition.
[2] Bashō's final poem. Dictated to approximately 60 disciples surrounding his deathbed.

# Takarai Kikaku    (1661–1707)[1]

### amagaeru / bashō ni norite / soyogi keri

The tree frog
Rides on a banana leaf—
How it sways!
NGS

### kojiki kana / tenchi no kitaru / natsu goromo

There a beggar goes!
        Heaven and earth he's wearing
            for his summer clothes.
HGH

### yū suzumi / yoku zo otoko ni / umare keri[2]

Out enjoying the
Evening cool. How good to be
A he, not a she.
EGS

---

[1] Most admired of the "Ten Philosophers" or "Ten Wise Men," as Bashō's favorite disciples were called. He was 14 when he joined 39-year-old Bashō's inner circle.
[2] In summer heat, men were free to strip half-naked. Women had to be more modest.

*meigetsu ya / tatami no ue ni / matsu no kage*[1]

What a beautiful moon! It casts
The shadow of pine boughs upon the mats.

AM

*inazuma ya / kinō wa higashi / kyō wa nishi*[2]

the lightning . . .
yesterday in the east
today in the west

WJH

*kiraretaru / yume wa makoto ka / nomi no ato*[3]

that dream I had
        of being stabbed — was for real!
Bitten by a flea.

SDC

Stabbed in a dream —
Or was it reality?
The marks of a flea.

DK

---

[1] Considered by scholars to be a Kikaku masterpiece, for indicating the intense brightness of the full moon (harvest moon) casting soft shadows on the straw-grass mat (*tatami*) flooring.
[2] *See* Bashō, note 1, p. 16 (*re*: "lightning").
[3] Kikaku's most famous verse.

*kusa no to ni / ware wa tade kū / hotaru kana*[1]

At a grass hut I eat smartweed, I'm that kind of firefly

HS

*asagao ni / ware wa meshi kū / otoko kana*[2]

A man that eats
        his meal amidst morning glories
that's what I am!

SDC

*waga yuki to / omoeba karushi / kasa no ue*

"It's my snow"
I think
And the weight on my hat lightens.

AK

---

[1] *Tade* is smartweed, knotweed or knotgrass. Thorny and stinging, it is spurned by insects, except for summer fireflies. Kikaku, who was a rich doctor's spoiled son, debauched with heavy drinking and whoremongering, here likens himself to the brilliant firefly that stays up all night enjoying the bitterness and dangers of overindulgence and promiscuity. The poem refers to the proverb "some prefer nettles . . ."

[2] Bashō's reply to the above poem is a rebuke, meaning he prefers a simple life contemplating nature. When other poets found Kikaku "incomprehensible," Bashō called him "swaggeringly elegant." He intended the remark as a compliment.

# Hattori Ransetsu    (1654–1707)[1]

*ume ichirin / ichirin hodo no / atatakasa*[2]

On the plum tree
      one blossom, one blossomworth
          of warmth
             HGH

*hitoha chiru / totsu hitoha chiru / kaze no ue*[3]

A leaf whirls down, alackaday!
A leaf whirls down upon the breeze.
               BHC

A leaf falls;
*Totsu!* a leaf falls,
on the wind.
     WJH

---

[1] Another of the "Ten Philosophers" or "Wise Men."

[2] The plum tree, harbinger of spring, flowers before its green leaves appear.

[3] Just as "blossom," when not modified, means cherry flower in haiku, "one leaf" is code for *kiri*. *Kiri*, a member of the figwort family, is the Pawlonia or Empress tree, named after the daughter of Tsar Paul I of Russia (1754–1801). A fast grower, it reaches a height of 20 feet in two seasons. The faintly perfumed wood is used in making clogs and clothes chests. The leaves drop throughout the year. They shrivel, turn yellow, and yield to gravity. Their falling symbolizes loneliness and connotes the past. The large purple flowers in early autumn are deeply associated with haiku because the three prongs hold 5, 7 and 5 buds respectively (*see* title-page illustration). The blooms and their bracket of leaves form the crest of the Empress of Japan. *Totsu* is an exclamation supposedly uttered when a Zen student achieves enlightenment. The sound also imitates the dry crackle the pawlonia leaf makes as it scratches the ground upon falling.

# Mukai Kyorai    (1651–1704)[1]

*hototogisu / naku ya hibari no / jūmonji*[2]

The cuckoo sings
at right angles
to the lark

BW

Listen! The cuckoos
Are calling—they and the skylarks
Make a crossmark.

DK

*nanigoto zo / hana miru hito no / nagagatana*[3]

A sabre! what has such to do
On one who comes to view the flowers?

BHC

# Kosugi Isshō    (1652–1688)[4]

*mi tsukushita / me wa shiragiku ni / modori keri*

My eyes, which had seen all, came back,
Back to the white chrysanthemums.

AM

[1] Another of the "Ten Wise Men."
[2] A skylark ascends vertically in quick flight. The *hototogisu* slowly takes off horizontally. When their orbits cross, the sight makes the ideogram for "ten" (+).
[3] A comment on armed samurai intruding on commoners' flower-viewing revels.
[4] A tea merchant and friend of Bashō.

# Ochi Etsujin    (1656–1739)[1]

*kimi ga haru / kaya wa moyogi ni / kiwamarinu*[2]

Spring in His Majesty's reign —
A mosquito net is light green
Throughout the ages.

MU

*yuku toshi ya / oya ni shiraga o / kakushi keri*[3]

The departing year
from my parents I have kept
my grey hair hidden.

BLE

# Shida Yaba    (1663–1740)[4]

*hottoba no / kaki yori uchi wa / sumire kana*[5]

Behold! violets bloom within
The fence of the forbidden ground.

AM

---

[1] Another of Bashō's "Ten Wise Men."
[2] Even today, mosquito nets large enough to encase a whole bedroom are always a "faded" light green, a color that supposedly repels insects. Bashō removed the patriotism by changing the opening line to "the moon's rays" (*tsuki kage ya*).
[3] Etsujin, a favored disciple 12 years Bashō's junior, did not write this *hokku* out of vanity (i.e. trying to appear young), but rather to express filial piety by *not* wishing to remind his parents of *their* growing old.
[4] One of the "Ten Wise Men."
[5] A protest verse: Nature is free to ignore a Lord's fiat. Violets in Japan lack scent and are considered a lovely but humble "grass."

*hakisōji / shite kara tsubaki / chirini keri*[1]

After I've swept and tidied up,
Adown fall some camellias.

BHC

*hototogisu / kao no dasarenu / kōshi kana*[2]

*hototogisu* —
can't get my head
through the lattice

WJH

## Kagami Shikō    (1665–1731)[3]

*soko moto wa / suzushisō nari / mine no matsu*

Even though afar,
A feeling of coolness comes
From those mountain pines.

GWB

*urayamashi / utsukushū natte / chiri momiji*[4]

How I envy maple leafage
which turns beautiful and then falls!

AM

---

[1] Camellia, a winter flower, falls all at once, not petal by petal. Haiku poets likened it to a head being severed by a samurai sword.

[2] At the sound of the *hototogisu*, Yaba rushed to the window, but the crossbars were too small for him to stick his head out and catch sight of the bird.

[3] A disciple of Bashō's, and pupil of Onitsura. *See* Onitsura, note 4, p. 37.

[4] With the first frost, maple leaves change color — become beautiful then fall — unlike the drab decline of human beings.

# Tachibana Hokushi   (ca. 1665–1718)[1]

### *yakeni keri / saredomo hana wa / chiri sumashi*[2]

My house burned down
But anyway, it was after
The flower petals had already fallen.

AK

### *karakasa no / ikutsu sugiyuku / yuki no kure*

'Twas a snowy evening.
How many umbrellas went by?

AM

### *botan chitte / kokoro mo okazu / wakare keri*[3]

The peony flowers having fallen,
We part without regrets.

AM

---

[1] Another of the "Ten Wise Men."
[2] When Hokushi's house burned down a second time, Shikō sent him an "imitative" poem:

> *yakeni keri / saredomo sakura / sakanu uchi*
> You are burnt out, but luckily
> Before the cherry-flowers bloom   AM

[3] After watching the peony petals wilt and scatter, Hokushi let his friend, the poet Shisui, leave for Edo without further regret at parting.

*kaite mitari / keshitari hate wa / keshi no hana*[1]

I write, I look, I erase
And in the end
A poppy of erasure.

AK

# Nozawa Bonchō   (d. 1714)[2]

*naganaga to / kawa hito suji ya / yuki no hara*

A single river stretching far
Across the moorland swathed in snow.

BHC

*mono no oto / hitori taoruru / kagashi kana*

A sound of something! the scarecrow
Has fall'n down of itself.

AM

[1] Hokushi's deathbed poem, containing a pun on *keshi* which means both "to erase" and "poppy," whose petals easily leave their stem. The double meaning is that when a poet corrects himself he arrives at a better poem. Also, having lived a life of trying to write well, he will now die content.

[2] Bonchō, Bashō's disciple and "an impoverished doctor," was convicted of smuggling, a crime punishable by having one's nose cut off. Because of his reputation as a poet, he was exiled instead.

*kiri no ki no / kaze ni kamawanu / ochiba kana*[1]

When no wind at all
    disturbs the kiri tree —
        the leaves that fall!

               HGH

*washi no su no / kusu no kare e ni / hi wa irinu*[2]

At an eagle's nest on dead camphor branches, the sun goes
down

    HS

## Yamamoto Kakei    (1648–1716)[3]

*tsuta no ha ya / nokorazu ugoku / aki no kaze*

Leaves of ivy
    Every one astir —
The autumn wind

        SHJ

*tsuma nashi to / yanushi ya kureshi / ominaeshi*[4]

I have no wife, said I.
    And so my landlord gave to me
A tiny maiden flower.

        SHJ

[1] *See* Ransetsu, note 3, p. 28 (*re*: Pawlonia tree).

[2] Generally considered Bonchō's masterpiece. It paints a vast canvas: the sun is high on a mountainside in the far distance and a huge camphor tree with sprawling black branches cradles a great bird's nest.

[3] A Bashō disciple.

[4] *See* Bashō, note 2, p. 18 (*re: ominaeshi*).

# Ogawa Haritsu    (1662–1747)[1]

*tsuma ni mo to / ikutari omou / hana mi kana*

I find so many
fit to be my wife
at flower-viewing time!

FB

# Sanboku

*toriyagebaba ga / migi no te nari no / momiji kana*[2]

How like it is to
A midwife's right hand —
Crimson maple leaf!

MU

# Kawai Otokuni[3]

*mushi yo mushi yo / naite inga ga / tsukiru nara*[4]

O, insect! — think you that
Karma can be exhausted by song?

LH

---

[1] A lacquerer and pupil of Bashō.
[2] In 1672 Bashō awarded this stanza, despite its 7-7-5 form, a prize in a *renga* contest, calling its conceit unique. Nothing else is known about Sanboku, nor do any of his other poems exist.
[3] Dates unknown, but he was a Bashō pupil. *See* Chigetsu, note 1, p. 41.
[4] *See* Bashō, note 2, p. 17 (*re: semi* and *mushi* ["bug"]).

## Anonymous    (belonging to Bashō's period)

### *sono ato wa / meido de kikan / hototogisu*[1]

> The rest of your song
> I'll hear in the Other World
>     Oh, sweet cuckoo bird!
>                    TGT

### *tsumu mo oshi / tsumanu mo oshiki / sumire kana*

I regret picking
and not picking
violets
    FB

### *chō wa mina / jūshichi hachi no / sugata kana*

> You butterflies all
> Are youthfulness incarnate
>     Like teens in their prime!
>                    TGT

---

[1] As a condemned criminal was about to be beheaded, a *hototogisu* sang sadly. The executioners recorded his farewell words. *See* Sōin, note 2, p. 9.

# Den Sute-jo    (1634–1698)[1]

*yuki no asa / ni no ji ni no ji no / geta no ato*[2]

Morning snow: figure two figure two wooden clog marks

HS

*higurashi ya / sutete oite mo / kururu hi wa*[3]

Cicada!
Not your doing
But day darkens . . .

FB

# Uejima Onitsura    (1661–1738)[4]

*koi koi to / iedo hotaru ga / tonde yuku*[5]

Although I say,
   "Come here! Come here!" the fireflies
      keep flying away!

HGH

---

[1] The very *haikai* pen name "Sute-jo" means "abandoned" or "thrown away" woman.

[2] Said to have been written when she was six. The two supports of Japanese wooden clogs leave an imprint like the ideogram for two (=).

[3] *Higurashi* (literally "day darkener"), is a sweet-voiced insect that sings *kana-kana-kana* at twilight. *See* Bashō, note 2, p. 17.

[4] One of the four greatest haiku writers. He was the third son of a well-to-do saké brewer and, from age 16, a pupil of Sōin. Teacher of Shikō. (*See* p. 31). Onitsura lifted *haikai*, which had been in decline both before and after Bashō, from "the level of a party game . . . [He] elevated it from a low-culture form to high culture," according to Cheryl Crowley. Onitsura was a little younger than Bashō but just as famous.

[5] First poem, written at age eight.

*gyōzui no / sutedokoro naki / mushi no koe*[1]

No place
to throw out the bathwater —
sound of insects

CAC

*amagumo no / ume o hoshi to mo / hiru nagara*

Under the rainclouds
The plum blossoms seem like stars
Despite the daylight.

CAC

*sakura saku koro / tori ashi nihon / uma shihon*[2]

When cherry trees bloom
birds have two legs
horses four

FB

[1] Onitsura is best known for this haiku. Compare it with Chiyo-jo's celebrated morning-glory poem (p. 44) for showing a sensitive deference to nature. *Gyōzui* is an outdoor, hot-water bath commoners took in their gardens during the heat of summer. By introducing a melancholy symbol of autumn, the chirping of cicadas, the poet is saying goodbye to one season and accepting the next. This verse was so wildly popular, it invited a famous parody:

> *onitsura wa / yachū tarai o / mochi aruki*
> Onitsura
> Walked around all night
> A pail in his hand   DK

[2] Note the 7-7-5 form. Harold Henderson called this "a shout of joy!" The perfection of flowers reawakens the poet's astonishment at the obvious. Onitsura's great insight (*satori*) was, he said, "There is no *haikai* without *makoto*." *Makoto* is truth, sincerity or "the absence of falsehood." He called it the "Way of Heaven," and added that "yearning for *makoto*" is the Way of Human Beings.

*gaikotsu no / ue o yosōte / hanami kana*[1]

Oh! flower-gazers, who have decked
the surface of their skeletons!

BHC

*hitokuwa ya / oshiki ni noseshi / sumiregusa*[2]

One stroke of the hoe —
they huddle, uprooted
the violets

CAC

*teizen ni / shiroku saitaru / tsubaki kana*[3]

In the garden, see
Near us, blossoming whitely,
The camellia-tree!

HGH

---

[1] Underneath finery, all men are the same "100 bones and 9 orifices"; their lives, too, are as brief as a cherry blossom's.

[2] Violets bloom in late spring and are so tiny they are scarcely noticeable. *See* Yaba, note 5, p. 30.

[3] A Zen priest posed Onitsura an unanswerable question (*kōan*), such as, "What is the sound of one hand clapping?" or "What color is the wind?" When he asked Onitsura, "What is *haikai*?," Onitsura replied with this well-known verse. In Buddhism, whiteness leads to absolute purity or enlightenment (*satori*). White, not black, is also the color associated with death.

*nyoppori to / aki no sora naru / fuji no yama*

Towering alone
against the autumn sky—
Mount Fuji

CAC

*akikaze no / fukiwatari keri / hito no kao*

The autumn wind
blowing across
people's faces

CAC

*kono aki wa / hiza ni ko no nai / tsukimi kana*[1]

This autumn
I'll be looking at the moon
With no child on my knee.

DK

*kakemeguru / yume ya yake no no / kaze no oto*[2]

Wandering dreams. Alas!
Over fields all burned, the winds
Whisper as they pass!

HGH

[1] Written on the death of his eldest son at age six, in 1700.
[2] *Hokku* composed at the memorial gathering on the 13th anniversary of Bashō's death. *See* Bashō, p. 24 (*re*: death poem).

*atataka ni / fuyu no hinata no / samuki kana*

A warm day,
But there's a chill
In the winter sun.

NGS

*nani yue ni / naga mijika aru / tsurara zo ya*

For some reason
There are long, and there are short
Icicles

AK

## Chigetsu    (ca. 1634–1708)[1]

*uguisu ni / temoto yasumenu / nagashi moto*[2]

Bush warbler: I rest my hands in the kitchen sink

HS

[1] Although some deplored *haikai* for becoming "a pastime even for low-born women and children," many great women poets emerged in the Tokugawa Era, as they had with classical poetry. Chigetsu adopted her brother Otokuni (*see* p. 35) as her son, and both brother-son and mother studied haiku under Bashō.

[2] *Uguisu* is often translated as "nightingale," for its more poetic connotations in English. It is a quick-moving, sparrow-sized bird with a dusky-brown head and dusty white throat and chest. Its spring song—*hoiho-hokekyo*—is incomparably sweet, although its winter call is a coarser *chut-chut*. *Uguisu* sings in daylight during the spring of which it, along with plum blossoms, is a harbinger. Chigetsu was so enraptured by the bird's song that she stopped her morning chores of dish washing and cleaning vegetables.

# Shōfū-ni (1669–1758)[1]

*haikai no / sode mo bashō mo / kareno kana*[2]

Both the haikai sleeve and the plantain withered in the field

HS

# Ogawa Shūshiki (1669–1725)[3]

*idobata no / sakura abunashi / sake no ei*[4]

The cherry by the well is dangerous for one drunken on wine

HS

*mishi yume no / samete mo iro no / kakitsubata*[5]

Even after waking
From the dream
I'll see the colors of irises.

AK

[1] Bashō gave this woman her *haikai* name, Shōfū or "treetop wind." *Ni* indicates that, in samurai custom, she shaved her head and became a nun after her husband's death.

[2] This haiku laments Bashō's passing as the withering of his beloved banana (plantain) plant (*bashō*). She also sewed clothes for Bashō and his followers, inventing the famous "*haikai* sleeve," where the right arm of the kimono was an inch shorter than the left, thereby making calligraphy easier. It also accented the eccentric appearance that *haikai* writers flaunted.

[3] Wife of a cookie-shop owner.

[4] Written when she was 13 years old. Is the drunk man in danger of crashing into the fragile flowering tree, or might he fall down the well?

[5] This was Shūshiki's death poem, meaning that when she awakens from "life's dream" she will see radiant irises. *Kakitsubata* or rabbit-eared iris, is another five-syllable word favored in haiku. The intensely purple petals were used as dye-stuff, their color being associated with young girls. Bashō's contemporary Ogata Kōrin (1661–1716) painted a screen of irises that became as internationally famous as Monet's water-lilies.

# Takeda [Tome] Ukō-ni    (1687–1743)[1]

*waga ko nara / tomo ni wa yaraji / yoru no yuki*

If my child, I wouldn't let him go with you in tonight's snow

HS

*nuimono ya / ki mo sede yogosu / satsuki ame*

the sewing . . .
unworn yet soiled . . .
midsummer rain

WJH

# Kaga no Chiyo    (1703–1775)[2]

*hototogisu / hototogisu tote / akeni keri*[3]

While I was musing on my theme,
Repeating "cuckoo," day has dawned.

AM

---

[1] Wife of Bonchō (*see* p. 33) and sister of Kyorai (*see* p. 29). On a wintry, slippery night Bonchō, with his 12-year-old servant boy, was about to leave for a *haikai no renga* party. Ukō recited this poem on the spur of the moment. Bonchō, awed and ashamed, went on alone.

[2] Also known as Chiyo-jo, to indicate a married woman, and later Chiyo-ni, to show she had become a nun. Chiyo is one of the most popularly beloved haiku poetesses although, until recently, scholars had reviled her as "pretentious," "sentimental" and "provincial and didactic."

[3] As a young girl, she asked a well-known poet for lessons in *hokku*. He assigned her the most common, yet most difficult subject, *hototogisu*, and then rudely went into the next room to sleep. At dawn, she handed him this "perfect" verse. The master was humiliated by a child.

Cuckoo!
Again cuckoo!
Again the daylight too!

CHP

*asagao ni / tsurube torarete / moraimizu*[1]

All round the rope a morning-glory clings
How can I break its beauty's dainty spell?
I beg for water from a neighbor's well.

CMW

morning glory!
the well-bucket entangled,
I ask for water.

PD & YI

The well-ladle is claimed
by the morning glories that twine it
So I beg water elsewhere

EM

*koe nakuba / sagi ushinawamu / kesa no yuki*[2]

but for their voices
the herons would disappear —
this morning's snow

PD & YI

---

[1] This verse is as widely known as Bashō's frog-pond opus. Compare it with Onitsura's bathwater-insect haiku, for delicate reluctance to disturb nature. *See* Onitsura, p. 38.

[2] *See* Sōkan, p. 4 (*re*: heron-snow haiku).

*beni saita / kuchi mo wasururu / shimizu kana*[1]

rouged lips
forgotten —
clear spring water

> PD & YI

I forgot my lips are rouged, at the clear water

> HS

*yūgao ya / onago no hada no / miyuru toki*[2]

moon flowers!
when a woman's skin
is revealed

> PD & YI

*wakakusa ya / kirema kirema ni / mizu no iro*[3]

green grass —
between, between the blades
the color of water

> PD & YI

[1] When she is about to bend down and drink from a spring of perfectly clear water, she forgets her lipstick will briefly stain the water's purity. Alternately, when she is about to mix *beni* (safflower) dye with water to make cheek rouge and lip coloring, the water is so crystal clear she hesitates to defile it with her vanity.

[2] She finds her naked skin as white and translucent as soft petals of the evening-glory flower (*Convulvulus*).

[3] The dew glistens clearly despite the green of the grass.

### *tsukubōte / kumo o ukagau / kaeru kana*

squatting
the frog observes
the clouds
PD & YI

### *akikaze no / yama o mawaru ya / kane no koe*

the autumn wind
resounds in the mountain —
temple bell
PD & YI

### *somekanete / kata yama momiji / kata omoi*[1]

No autumn colors tint that side of the mountain: a one-sided
love
JB

### *akebono no / wakare wa motanu / hiina kana*[2]

dawn's separation
unknown
to dolls
PD & YI

---

[1] The frost of autumn has not yet tinted the leaves on the sunny, unsheltered side of the mountain. Her description of unrequited love.

[2] Dolls never know the loneliness of early morning when a woman's lover has left after a night of love.

*torikage mo / ha ni mite sabishi / fuyu no tsuki*

leaves like bird shadows
desolate —
the winter moon
　　　PD & YI

mistaking birds for leaves — lonely, a winter's moon
　　　　　　　　　　　　　　　　　　HS

---

*shimizu suzushi / hotaru no kiete / nani mo nashi*[1]

clear water is cool
fireflies vanish —
there's nothing more
　　　PD & YI

---

*chōchō ya / nani o yume mite / hanezukai*[2]

The butterfly —
What are the dreams that make him
Flutter his wings?
　　　DK

---

[1] Nothing disturbs the silent tranquility of the moment.
[2] A reference to Chuang Tsu (Zhuangzi). *See* Sōin, note 1, p. 10.

### *okite mitsu / nete mitsu kaya no / hirosa kana*[1]

I sleep . . . I wake . . .
   How wide
The bed with none beside.

CHP

### *tombo tsuri / kyō wa doko made / itta yara*[2]

I wonder in what fields today
He chases dragonflies in play
My little boy who ran away.

CHP

Chasing dragonflies
Today what place is it
he has strayed off to?

EM

---

[1] Believed to have been written by Chiyo who, married at 19, was widowed eight years later. So famous was this poem it inspired a bawdy parody:

> If your mosquito-net is too large,
> Shall I share it with you, O-Chiyo?

The mosquito-net haiku above was written by Ukihashi, a courtesan of the pleasure district.

[2] Japanese boys catch dragonflies by attaching gum to the tip of a bamboo pole, like a fishing rod. This haiku, one of the most moving in literature, was written by Chiyo after her only child died at the age of nine.

*hana sakanu / mi wa kurui yoki / yanagi kana*[1]

With no flowers
You are free as a willow.

FB

*hyaku nari mo / tsuru hitotsu ji no / kokoro yori*[2]

A hundred different gourds
From the mind
Of one vine.

RHB

*tsuki mo mite / ware wa kono yo o / kashiku o kana*[3]

I've seen the moon
I sign my letter to the world
"Respectfully yours"

FB

---

[1] A sympathetic friend sent Chiyo a *hokku* on the loss of both her husband and child, invoking the old adage "the willow need not regret having no flowers." Chiyo replied:

> Without flowers
> one leads as quiet a life
> as the willow tree

Chiyo meant that the willow is not bothered with flower-viewers or by storms that buffet other trees' leaves. Her answer is something of a rebuff to her friend's well-meant condolence.

[2] When Chiyo asked to enter a nunnery the Zen master, who considered poetry "a worldly attachment," asked her how *haikai* could be Zen-worthy (i.e. have a thousand meanings from a single thought). The master was humbled by the excellence of this haiku, and accepted her into his order.

[3] Chiyo-ni's deathbed verse. *Kashiku* is an elegant woman's phrase to conclude formal letters.

# Hayano Hajin    (1677–1742)[1]

*shirafuji ya / kaze ni fukaruru / ama no gawa*

Behold the white wistarias —
The Milky Way blown by the wind.

AM

*sumigama ya / shika no mite iru / yūkemuri*[2]

The charcoal kiln —
A deer watches
The evening smoke

DK

# Gozan    (1695–1733)

*ka ya hiraki / nori toku tori no / kirabiyaka*[3]

The wonder of
flowers opening
and birds singing:
prayers!

FB

---

[1] Pupil of Kikaku and Ransetsu and teacher of Buson (*see* p. 52). Important poet in the 1730's "Back to Bashō" movement.

[2] Farmers used smoke as a repellent to keep deer from despoiling their fields.

[3] This *haikai* trickery, a palindrome, reads the same forward and backward in *kana* (the Japanese alphabet).

# Tan Taigi    (1709–1771)

### yabuiri no / neru ya hitori no / oya no soba

Servant day
sleeping — near
the lone parent

WJH

### degawari ya / tatami e otosu / namida kana[1]

The change of servants
Her tears
Splash on the tatami

AM

# Yagi Shokyū-ni    (1713–1781)[2]

### wasuregusa wa / sakedo wasure nu / mukashi kana[3]

The "forget-me" has bloomed, but ah!
I can not forget old days together.

AM

---

[1] Once a year Japanese traditionally allowed their household servants and menials to return to their own homes briefly (*yabuiri*). *Degawari* was the day, after six months' service, apprentices advanced to new jobs, and old servants were retired.

[2] Wife of Shida Yaba's secretary. *See* Yaba, p. 30.

[3] Written on the 13th anniversary of her husband's death. *Wasuregusa* (literally, "forget-me-grass") is a tiny, ephemeral day-lily.

*shiraga to mo / narade yanagi no / chiri ni keri*[1]

Lo! willow leaves have gone,
Without getting grey-haired.

AM

*yakeshi no no / tokorodokoro ya / sumiregusa*[2]

Violets have grown here and there
on the ruins of my burned house.

AM

## Yosa Buson    (1716–1783)[3]

*bashō sarite / sono nochi imada / toshi kurezu*[4]

Bashō departed
And since then
The year has never ended.

AK

---

[1] Willows shed their leaves without turning color or shriveling. Shokyū-ni envies them as she is losing her beauty in old age. *See* note 4, p. 31.

[2] Compare other haiku about violets. *See* Yaba, p. 30 and Onitsura, p. 39.

[3] One of the four greatest haiku poets, an even greater painter and a master of vivid images. The name *Buson* can be written either as "deserted village" or "turnip village." He was born near Osaka, in a place famous for sweet turnips. Buson was first a disciple of Kikaku, although he found that master's *hokku* so obscure as to be like "wearing brocade on a pitch-black night." At age 22, in 1737, he became Hajin's pupil and was active in the "Back to Bashō" movement that restored haiku to legitimacy after a period of 50 years' decline. Some of Buson's longer poems read like twentieth-century free verse. He was passionate about Kabuki and the "world of flowers and willows," and used his poems, calligraphy and paintings to pay for tickets and prostitutes.

[4] This is one of several homages to the "Venerable Bashō," as is the next *hokku* (page 53).

*furuike no / kawazu oiyuku / ochiba kana*

In an old pond a frog ages while leaves fall

TR

*haru no umi / hinemosu notari / notari kana*[1]

The spring sea swells and falls, and swells—
Until the bell of tardy evening knells.

SN

*harusame ya / monogatari yuku / mino to kasa*[2]

Springtime rain: together
       intent upon their talking, go
              straw-raincoat and umbrella

HGH

*tenteki ni / utarete komoru / katatsumuri*

struck by a
raindrop, snail
closes up.

JBe

---

[1] Written at Matsushima, where he followed Bashō's footsteps. This haiku is considered a masterpiece of gently undulating onomatopoeia, matching in sound the sight of the sea circling around the pine-tree islands.

[2] Buson's most noted haiku, but it is a mystery. Who are they? Two men? A man and a woman? What are they saying? *Mino* are worn by country folk, and *kasa* are carried by city people. The discrepancy adds to the puzzle of two unlikely people sharing the same rainy moment.

### *kaze ichijin / mizutori shiroku / miyuru kana*[1]

A gust of wind, —
And the waterbirds
    Become white.

RHB

### *yūkaze ya / mizu aosagi no / hagi o utsu*[2]

The evening breezes —
The water splashes against
A blue heron's shins.

DK

### *fundoshi senu / shiri fukareyuku / haru no kaze*

There's no loincloth
    on that butt blown in view —
in the spring breeze.

SDC

---

[1] When ruffled, a waterfowl's underfeathers show white.
[2] Donald Keene calls this haiku a *"tour de force."* Buson himself felt he had at last attained his ideal with this stanza.

*mishi koi no / chigo neriide yo / dōkuyō*[1]

> to see him was to love
> if only he would come out again
> for the temple rites

EM

Acolyte I love, march out for the hall service

HS

*shigururu ya / ware mo kojin no / yo ni nitaru*[2]

overcome by this cold falling rain:
how very similar, my life
to my old friend's

SG & SS

*yo ni furu mo / sara ni sōgi no / yadori kana*[3]

long my labors and no longer young
I remain even now, like Sōgi on the move
from lodging to lodging

SG & SS

---

[1] Technically this is not a *hokku* since it lacks a *kigo* (seasonal word). *See also* Bashō, note 1, p. 23 (*re: chigo*).

[2] The "old friend" or "departed one" (*kojin*) is Sōgi (*see* p. 3).

[3] The emphasis in these two haiku is not only on the hardships traveling beggar-poets endured in their search for inspiration from the vicissitudes of nature, but also on their restless efforts to improve their art — their search for the perfect poem expressing precisely what they saw, thought, felt and meant.

*hototogisu / matsu ya miyako no / soradanome*[1]

For the cuckoo I wait
here in the capital beneath the vain skies of hoping

MM

*fuji hitotsu / uzumi nokoshite / wakaba kana*[2]

Fuji alone
remains unburied:
the young leaves!

WJH

*ochizama ni / mizu koboshi keri / hana tsubaki*[3]

Why, as it fell
Water that was in it spilled
Camellia bell!

HGH

[1] Buson headed this *hokku*: "I've lived in Kyoto (*miyako*) more than 20 years, but have only been fortunate to hear a *hototogisu* twice."

[2] Mt. Fuji, an extinct volcano, has greenery only at its base. Spring verdure surrounded the low-lying hills but Fuji itself was naked. Buson did not write the words for Mt. Fuji, but simply drew an instantly recognizable cone-shape and continued the poem in words.

[3] *See* Yaba, note 1, p. 31 (*re*: Camellia).

### *tsurigane ni / tomarite nemuru / kochō kana*[1]

On the great temple bell
stopped from flight and sleeping
the small butterfly

EM

### *niji o haite / hirakan to suru / botan kana*[2]

The peony bud,
When opening,
Shoots forth a rainbow.

NGS

### *botan chitte / uchi kasanarinu / ni sanpen*[3]

Peony petals fell
piling one upon another
in twos in threes

EM

[1] Cf. Amy Lowell (1874–1925) poem titled "Peace":

Perched upon the muzzle of a cannon
A yellow butterfly is slowly opening and shutting its wings

[2] The tree-peony, "King of Flowers," when its huge white buds open, reveals speckled red and black depths, like a Kabuki *kumadori* make-up.

[3] Most Japanese high-school students can recite this *hokku*, though few can explain its meaning. Fallen petals seemed to Buson as gorgeous as the full-blown flower. Buson wrote some 20 haiku on the subject of peonies.

*chirite nochi / omokage ni tatsu / botan kana*

After they've fallen,
their image remains in the mind—
those peonies
SDC

*nashi no hana / tsuki ni fumi yomu / onna ari*

A woman
Reading a letter by moonlight
Pear blossoms.
AK

*na no hana ya / tsuki wa higashi ni / hi wa nishi ni*[1]

Rape-flowers—
Eastward the moon,
Westward the sun.
NGS

---

[1] The rape plant, a close relative of wild mustard, is cultivated for rapeseed oil which is burned with cotton wicks for lamplight. Despite its unfortunate name in English, it is much admired by flower viewers for its forsythia-like wands of strident yellow flowers. Here, it is late afternoon and both the setting sun and the rising moon are visible over a golden carpet of rape flowers.

*yokohiki ya / inu no togamuru / hei no uchi*[1]

hunter out before dawn
a dog scolds him on the far side of the fence

MM

*musasabi no / kotori hamiiru / kareno kana*[2]

a flying squirrel sits chewing on a bird withered field

MM

*shiraume ni / akuru yo bakari to / narinikeri*[3]

For white plum blossoms, time has come for the day to break

HS

## Ōshima Ryōta    (1718–1787)[4]

*samidare ya / aru yo hisoka ni / matsu no tsuki*

All the rains of June:
    and one evening, secretly,
        through the pines, the moon.

HGH

[1] The barking will alert the prey, and the hunter, despite his stealth at this early hour, is deprived of hoped-for quarry.
[2] Buson's own favorite among his thousands of haiku.
[3] Buson's farewell and final poem (*jisei*).
[4] A pupil of Ransetsu and one of the first to "rediscover" Bashō. Donald Keene observes that Ryōta published 200 books of poems and attained 2,000 disciples but "hardly a single poem has survived the test of time."

*mono iwazu / kyaku to teishu to / shiragiku to*

Saying nothing:
Guest and host
and white chrysanthemum.

FB


## Tagami Kikusha-ni    (1753–1826)[1]

*tama ni ge ni / mokutō ya tada / michi no tsuki*

In spirit and in truth
silent prayer . . . just
the moon on the road

WJH

*ogami awan to / onaji kumoi no / tsuki hitotsu*[2]

Let's all adore
in the same well of clouds
this one moon

WJH


[1] A Buddhist nun and friend of Issa.
[2] The moon connotes "enlightenment" in Buddhism. "Well of clouds," according to William J. Higginson, is "the sky of this illusory world."

# Kobayashi Issa    (1763–1827)[1]

*ware to kite / asobe yo oya no / nai suzume*[2]

Oh, won't some orphan sparrow come and play with me.

MB

Come with me,
Let's play together, swallow
Without a mother.

DK

*mata muda ni / kuchi aku tori no / mamako kana*[3]

Once more in vain the stepchild bird opens its beak

MB

---

[1] Third of the four "Greats" of haiku. His father was a peasant farmer and packhorse hostler, in what we today call the Japan Alps. "Issa" literally means "one tea," indicating that life is as empty as froth on a cup of tea.

[2] Issa's mother died when he was two, still suckling at the breast. His grandmother asked neighbors and even passers-by to nurse the child for her. He claimed he wrote this masterpiece of pathos at age 6. He used the word "sparrow," however a picture Issa later drew to illustrate the poem shows a swallow.

[3] Issa's notoriously wicked stepmother often punished him by withholding food. In his famous autobiography he wrote, "I was beaten 100 times a day, 1,000 times a month, and in the 356 days of the [lunar] year, there was never one when my eyes were not swollen."

### *suzume no ko / soko noke soko noke / ōuma ga toru*[1]

Young sparrows, get out of the way!
    get out of the way!
        A great horse is coming by!
                AM

### *dokadoka to / hana no ue naru / bafun kana*

Thud-thud upon the flowers drops the horse turd
                HS

### *yare utsu na / hai ga te o suri / ashi o suru*

Hey! Don't swat:
the fly wrings his hands
on bended knees
        FB

### *yasegaeru / makeru na issa / kore ni ari*[2]

Puny frog
Don't give up
Issa's here!
    FB

---

[1] Issa is remembering his childhood when he rode a hobbyhorse outside his house, imitating the Great Lords (*daimyō*) preceded by their retainers shouting, "Make way!"

[2] Written on seeing two bullfrogs fight during mating season. Typically, Issa takes the side of the weakling.

*sumi no kumo / anjina susu o / toranu zo yo*[1]

Don't get alarmed, you corner spiders. I won't touch your webs.

MB

*kago no tori / chō o urayamu / metsuki kana*

Ah, the sad expression in the eyes of that caged bird—
        envying the butterfly!

LH

*kore hodo to / botan no shikata / suru ko kana*

   "The peony was as big as this,"
Says the little girl
    Opening her arms.

RHB

*haikai no / kuchisugi ni / sakura kana*[2]

Cherry blossoms made for haikai poets to exploit

MB

---

[1] Issa was a careless housekeeper, rarely sweeping the *tatami* or even putting away his night bedding (*futon*).
[2] A veiled attack on *haikai* poets who see flowers only as excuses for making pretty poems.

*hototogisu to / hito ni yobaruru / samusa kana*[1]

The coldness of being called a country bumpkin!

MB

*hana no kage / aka no tanin wa / nakari keri*

Under cherry-flowers,
None are utter strangers.

AM

*shitajita ni / umarete yoru mo / sakura kana*[2]

Being born the lowest of the low, I view cherries at night

MB

*etadera no / sakura majimaji / sakini keri*[3]

Cherries at the Eta Temple coweringly blossom

MB

---

[1] *Hototogisu*, because of its rarity in cities, became a mock-elegant epithet used by sophisticated townsmen to show contempt for countryfolk flocking to Edo during the Tokugawa period. Issa, who wrote movingly of farmers and peasant life, unlike some other haiku poets, never hid his origins although he was pained to be slurred as a *hototogisu* (cuckoo). See Sōin, note 2, p. 9.

[2] Unlike samurai, whose pleasures were more restricted, commoners could pass the whole night in flower-viewing revels.

[3] *Eta* were Japan's "untouchables," who worked in slaughterhouses, dealt in leather and performed despised work. They are now called *Burakumin*, a euphemism similar to that applied to the untouchable caste of India, whom Gandhi renamed *harijan* or "Children of God."

*daimyō o / uma kara orosu / sakura kana*

Lo! the cherry-blossoms have forced
    A daimio to dismount.
        AM

*hana min to / itaseba shita ni / shita ni kana*[1]

Just bent on viewing cherries when — "On your knees, on
    your knees!"
        MB

*uguisu ya / gozen e dete mo / onaji koe*

The nightingale sings in the same voice ever,
    Even before His Lordship.
        AM

*shi ni jitaku / itaseitase to / sakura kana*[2]

Get ready, get ready to die, the cherries say
        HS

Falling cherry petals say
Hurry, hurry
Thy preparedness for death
        IMu

[1] Even at flower-viewing time, when a Great Lord arrived, the lower classes were ordered to prostrate themselves on the ground.

[2] Life's brief moment on earth is like the cherry blossom's short, three-day loveliness.

*saotome ya / ko no naku hō e / uete yuku*[1]

See that peasant! She plants toward her crying child.

MB

*nomidomo ni / matsushima misete / nigasu zo yo*[2]

I'll show you fleas Matsushima, and then I'll let you go

MB

*hito chirari / kono ha mo chirari / horari kana*[3]

people scattered
the leaves too scattered
and spread

WJH

---

[1] Many scholars consider this to be "the greatest poem in the Japanese language." The mother, busy transplanting rice seedlings, dare not stop working, but her row of rice shoots becomes crooked as she is pulled by anxiety toward her baby's crying. She has laid the child on the grassy ridge between rice paddies.

[2] Issa, following Bashō's travel to Matsushima (*see* Bashō, p. 18), arrived infested with the travelers' usual lice and fleas, but marvels at the scenery before he sets about picking them off his body and shaking them from his clothes. *Domo* is a plural form for "people," not insects.

[3] Both people and leaves are caught in a sudden shower of autumn rain.

*kore kara wa / dai nippon to / yanagi kana*[1]

Henceforth,
Great Japan
and willows!

FB

*konna yo wa / tō ni mo aru ka / hototogisu*

Can China have
such a night as this
when the *hototogisu* sings?

FB

*shinkoku no / matsu o itoname / oroshiyabune*[2]

Look to the pines of our godly land! The oroshiya ships.

MB

[1] Issa's love of his country was particularly important at a time when foreigners were knocking at Japan's gates, and Japan herself was eyeing the mother-country of China for expansion.

[2] During Issa's lifetime (the nineteenth century), Japan was becoming aware of itself vis-a-vis the West. Russian (*oroshiya*) ships began calling at Japanese seaports, much to the isolationist Tokugawa government's alarm. Japan's sturdy pines (that do not bend in the wind) symbolized to Issa his country's defenses against outside forces. "Godly" (*shinkoku*) is "country of Shintō religion."

*kyō kara wa / nippon no gan zo / raku ni ne yo*[1]

From today you're Japanese geese! Sleep in peace.

MB

*korosare ni / kotoshi mo kita ya / oda no kari*[2]

This year again, they've come to be killed! Geese in the ricefields.

MB

*ku no shaba ya / hana ga hirakeba / hiraku tote*

Ours is a world of suffering,
Even if cherry-flowers bloom.

AM

*nadeshiko no / naze oreta zo yo / oreta zo yo*[3]

Why did the pink break, oh why did it break?

MB

---

[1] In winter, geese from Siberia migrate to Japan. They return home in spring.
[2] On the stupidity of geese in coming year after year only to be shot (for pillaging the paddies) and eaten.
[3] Written on the death of his son in 1819. Issa had six children, five of whom died in infancy. The sixth was born posthumously. The pink or daisy (*nadeshiko*) is a delicate potted plant symbolic of Japanese virtue.

*tsuyu no yo wa / tsuyu no yo nagara / sari nagara*[1]

Life is but the morning dew, bards say;
'Tis true, indeed, but well-a-day!

AM

The world of dew is, yes, a world of dew, but even so

HS

The world of dew
Is a world of dew, and yet
And yet . . .

DK

*tomokaku mo / anata makase no / toshi no kure*[2]

After all, after all
I commend myself and mine to you —
Now at the year's end

LM

[1] Issa's most famous haiku. Written a month after the death of his daughter in 1816.
[2] *Anata* (literally "you") means the Lord Buddha. At year's end, Japanese pay all their debts. Impoverished Issa was in despair, knowing he would be dunned.

*tarai kara / tarai ni utsuru / chimpunkan*[1]

Tub to tub
The whole journey
Just hub-bub!

LM

From one tub until moved into the other — it's all double
Dutch to me

MB

# Ōtomo Ōemaru    (1719–1805)[2]

*ou hito ni / akari o misuru / hotaru kana*

to a pursuer
the firefly gives a look
at its light

WJH

*gan wa mada / ochitsuite iru ni / okaeri ka*

The wild geese yet
Are content to stay —
And must you return

LM

---

[1] Issa's last poem, written at age 65 and found under his deathbed's pillow. He refers to baby's first bath upon birth and the final washing of the corpse. *Chimpunkan* was a colloquialism for what can't be understood. Max Bickerton, knowing Issa had heard Dutchmen speaking in Nagasaki (where foreigners were confined at the time), chose the phrase "double Dutch" to mean "jibberish," and to convey Issa's idea that all he had written was meaningless in the face of death's finality.

[2] Issa's devoted poet friend, and his senior by 44 years.

# Ichikawa Danjūrō V    (1741–1806)[1]

*ōtachi o / tsurizao ni shite / raku inkyo*

My long stage sword
I use as a fishing rod
In easy retirement.

AK

*kogarashi ni / ame motsu kumo no / yukue kana*[2]

Where are the rain-laden clouds bound
Borne on the wintry wind?

LK

# Sakurai Baishitsu    (1769–1852)[3]

*tsubaki ochi / tori naki tsubaki / mata ochiru*

a camellia falls —
cock-crow and another
camellia falls

WJH

[1] Celebrated Kabuki actor.
[2] His farewell poem, composed on his deathbed.
[3] Considered a master of "perfect *haikai* poetry." Much scorned by Shiki for his "use of technique, rather than sincerity."

*kaya tsureba / kà mo omoshiroshi / tsuki ni tobu*

When the mosquito-net is put up,
The mosquitoes look lovely, flying about in moonbeams.

AM

## Kubota Seifū-jo    (1783–1884)[1]

*osanago ya / hana o misete mo / kuchi o aku*

Lo! the baby opens its mouth
Even when 'tis shown a flower.

AM

## Masaoka Shiki    (1867–1902)[2]

*ki o tsumite / yo no ake yasuki / komado kana*[3]

the tree cut,
dawn breaks early
at my little window

JBe

---

[1] Wife of Shunkō, Issa's pupil.

[2] Father of the modern haiku and last of the historic four great haiku writers. Shiki was the son of a petty official in service to the *daimyō* of Matsuyama on Shikoku Island. When Shiki began teaching English in Matsuyama, he lodged at the palace. Shiki had been diagnosed with spinal tuberculosis in 1895, and was well aware that the disease would soon claim his life.

[3] A gardener removed a branch from the tree outside Shiki's bedroom skylight, so light could come in sooner.

*harukaze ni / o o hirogetaru / kujaku kana*

fanning out its tail
in the spring breeze,
see — a peacock!

JBe

*mihotoke ni / shini mukeoreba / tsuki suzushi*[1]

I've turned my back
On Buddha
How cool the moon!

AK

*kaki kueba / kane ga naru nari / hōryūji*[2]

I bite into a persimmon
and a bell resounds —
Hōryūji

JBe

[1] Written while staying in a temple guest room with an altar on the wall. He turns from it to gaze at the moonlight outside. Is he choosing beauty over religion?

[2] Most famous of all Shiki's 18,000 haiku. Hōryūji is the oldest extant wooden building in the world — a Buddhist temple and monastery founded at Nara in 607 A.D. Scholars still puzzle over the ambiguity of the poem: the "then" of the temple's antiquity; the "now" of the persimmon; the momentary "bite" and the long-lasting "eternity" of a huge temple bell's tolling. Orchards around Hōryūji are famous for their persimmons, whose astringent-sweet taste is frequently referred to by Shiki.

*harusame ya / kasa sashite miru / ezōshiya*[1]

spring rain
browsing under my umbrella
at the picture-book store

JBe

*ichihatsu no / ichirin shirōshi / haru no kure*[2]

this lone iris
white
in spring twilight

SG & SS

*hito iyashiku / ran no atai o / ronji keri*

Men are disgusting.
They argue over
The price of orchids.

AK

*mon shime ni / dete kiite oru / kawazu kana*

Coming out to close the gate I end up listening to frogs

HS

---

[1] Bookstores displayed their wares on sidewalk counters under awnings.
[2] *Ichihatsu* is a fleur-de-lis, a kind of iris. Shiki contrasts the radiantly white, single flower with the gathering darkness of evening.

*nemuran to su / nanji shizuka ni / hae o ute*

I'm trying to sleep —
go easy
when you swat flies
BW

*odoroku ya / yūgao ochishi / yowa no oto*[1]

Surprise!
a moonflower fell —
midnight sound
JBe

*waga suki no / kaki o kuwarenu / yamai kana*

unable to devour
these persimmons I adore
oh this illness of mine!
SG & SS

*yuki furu yo / shōji no ana o / mite areba*

snow's falling!
I see it through a hole
in the shutter . . .
JBe

---

[1] Japan has *asa-gao*, "morning face" or morning glory, *hi-gao*, "day face," noonflower or day lily, and *yū-gao*, "evening face" or moonflower.

*yuki no ie ni / nete iru to omou / bakari nite*

all I can think of
is being sick in bed
and snowbound . . .

JBe

*ikutabi mo / yuki no fukasa o / tazune keri*

again and again
I ask how high
the snow is

JBe

*keitō no / jūshi-go-hon mo / arinu beshi*[1]

Cockscomb—
I'm sure there are at least
Fourteen or fifteen stalks

DK

[1] This is considered Shiki's masterpiece. Cockscombs are a blazing, fire-colored plant with stalks that grow to a height of two feet, tall enough to be seen at the veranda edge by Shiki lying on his pallet. They cluster together so tightly that counting them is difficult. To most readers, the pathos lies in the contrast between the dying man and the sturdy life outside.

*haikai no / harawata miseru / kamiko kana*[1]

A paper kimono
shows the guts of
*haikai!*

FB

*yomei / ikubaku ka aru / yo mijikashi*

how much longer
is my life?
a brief night . . .

JBe

*kakikui no / hokku suki to / tsutau beshi*[2]

Tell them
I was a persimmon eater
who liked haiku

BW

---

[1] *Kamiko* was a thin, windproof outer kimono made of crushed paper treated with persimmon juice. Having taken vows of poverty, *haikai* poets of yore (before Shiki) fancied such inexpensive wear, and they could also write poems on their clothing as a kind of self-advertisement.

[2] Although Shiki put the word "haiku" into common parlance, here he used the now out-of-fashion word *hokku*.

*jōbutsu ya / yūgao no kao / hechima no he*[1]

Buddha-death:
the moonflower's face
the snake gourd's fart

JBe

*ototoi no / hechima no mizu mo / torazariki*

the loofah water
from day before yesterday
still not taken

WJH

*hechima saite / tan no tsumarishi / hotoke kana*[2]

The towel gourd has flowered:
here lies a man dead,
suffocated by phlegm

SG & SS

---

[1] *Jōbutsu* (literally, to become a buddha), means "to die in peace" or "to go to heaven." *Hechima*, a loofah sponge, snake gourd or towel gourd, was grown in Shiki's garden for medicinal purposes. Before it flowers or goes to seed, it yields a juice that thins mucus and eases spasms of coughing. Facing the moon of death, medicine is as useless as a plant's fart, a pun on *he*.

[2] These last two haiku, dictated to a disciple, show that his condition was hopeless. The gourd plant was allowed to flower — its life became the symbol of Shiki's death. Here, *hotoke* (Buddha) means one who has just died. Natsume Sōseki (1867–1916), the celebrated novelist (his likeness is on ¥1,000 notes), was in London when Shiki died. In mourning for his friend, he wrote:

*kiri ki naru / ichi ni ugoku ya / kage bōshi*
See how it hovers
In these streets of yellow fog,
A human shadow

Donald Keene interprets this as Sōseki's thinking he saw Shiki's shade "on its way to the Yellow Springs of the afterworld."

# DOVER · THRIFT · EDITIONS

## POETRY

THE CONGO AND OTHER POEMS, Vachel Lindsay. 96pp. 0-486-27272-9

EVANGELINE AND OTHER POEMS, Henry Wadsworth Longfellow. 64pp. 0-486-28255-4

FAVORITE POEMS, Henry Wadsworth Longfellow. 96pp. 0-486-27273-7

COMPLETE POEMS, Christopher Marlowe. 112pp. 0-486-42674-2

"TO HIS COY MISTRESS" AND OTHER POEMS, Andrew Marvell. 64pp. 0-486-29544-3

SPOON RIVER ANTHOLOGY, Edgar Lee Masters. 144pp. 0-486-27275-3

SELECTED POEMS, Claude McKay. 80pp. 0-486-40876-0

SONGS OF MILAREPA, Milarepa. 128pp. 0-486-42814-1

RENASCENCE AND OTHER POEMS, Edna St. Vincent Millay. 64pp. (Not available in Europe or the United Kingdom) 0-486-26873-X

SELECTED POEMS, John Milton. 128pp. 0-486-27554-X

CIVIL WAR POETRY: An Anthology, Paul Negri (ed.). 128pp. 0-486-29883-3

ENGLISH VICTORIAN POETRY: AN ANTHOLOGY, Paul Negri (ed.). 256pp. 0-486-40425-0

GREAT SONNETS, Paul Negri (ed.). 96pp. 0-486-28052-7

THE RAVEN AND OTHER FAVORITE POEMS, Edgar Allan Poe. 64pp. 0-486-26685-0

ESSAY ON MAN AND OTHER POEMS, Alexander Pope. 128pp. 0-486-28053-5

GOBLIN MARKET AND OTHER POEMS, Christina Rossetti. 64pp. 0-486-28055-1

CHICAGO POEMS, Carl Sandburg. 80pp. 0-486-28057-8

CORNHUSKERS, Carl Sandburg. 157pp. 0-486-41409-4

COMPLETE SONNETS, William Shakespeare. 80pp. 0-486-26686-9

SELECTED POEMS, Percy Bysshe Shelley. 128pp. 0-486-27558-2

AFRICAN-AMERICAN POETRY: An Anthology, 1773–1930, Joan R. Sherman (ed.). 96pp. 0-486-29604-0

NATIVE AMERICAN SONGS AND POEMS: An Anthology, Brian Swann (ed.). 64pp. 0-486-29450-1

SELECTED POEMS, Alfred Lord Tennyson. 112pp. 0-486-27282-6

AENEID, Vergil (Publius Vergilius Maro). 256pp. 0-486-28749-1

GREAT LOVE POEMS, Shane Weller (ed.). 128pp. 0-486-27284-2

CIVIL WAR POETRY AND PROSE, Walt Whitman. 96pp. 0-486-28507-3

SELECTED POEMS, Walt Whitman. 128pp. 0-486-26878-0

THE BALLAD OF READING GAOL AND OTHER POEMS, Oscar Wilde. 64pp. 0-486-27072-6

EARLY POEMS, William Carlos Williams. 64pp. (Available in U.S. only.) 0-486-29294-0

FAVORITE POEMS, William Wordsworth. 80pp. 0-486-27073-4

EARLY POEMS, William Butler Yeats. 128pp. 0-486-27808-5